To all the children who will read this book, may it fill your hearts with joy and inspire you to be the best version of yourselves. You are unique, you are special, and you are loved just the way you are.

Always embrace your individuality and remember that your differences make you shine bright like stars. Let this book be a gentle reminder that you are capable of achieving anything you set your mind to, and that your dreams are within reach.

Believe in yourselves, and
let your light shine into the world.

With love,
Taylor & Latoya

Text copyright © Latoya Baldwin, Taylor Baldwin,
Books & Things Publishing, LLC 2023
Illustrations copyright © Sarah Jane Docker 2023

All rights reserved. No part of this publication may be reproduced, distributed, or transmitted in any form without prior written permission.

ISBN: 978-1-7358842-2-6 (Paperback)
ISBN: 978-1-7358842-1-9 (Hardcover)

Library of Congress Control Number: 2023918609

Any references to historical events, real people, or real places are used fictitiously. Names, characters, and places are products of the author's imagination.

First published in 2023
Formatted by Dennis Rivera

Books & Things Publishing, LLC
4410 Brookfield Corporate Dr. #220149 Chantilly, VA 20153
www.booksandthingspublishing.com

written by
LaToya & Taylor Baldwin

illustrated by
Sarah Jane Docker

Kiara and her Invisible Crown

My name is Kiara and I really **don't** like being called a princess.

Nothing against princesses or anything, I think they're great!

But wearing a crown and pink fluffy dresses and dancing in a ballroom waiting for a prince just isn't me.

I prefer **other** things, you know?

I love playing the guitar and my friends would definitely call me a gamer.

I would choose the color blue over the color pink any day – it reminds me of how my favorite aunt wears her police uniform with pride every day.

What will I be when I grow up? Just you **wait and see**…

I love everything that a **princess** surely would **not**.

Like I do, all girls have different interests. Sometimes, adults don't realize that and assume we all like the same things.

For my family, that idea was about to change... thanks to me!

On the day of my grandma's birthday, my whole family was meeting up at her house to celebrate and all I could think of were **two** things:

First...of course, cake.
And second, I hope that no one calls me **princess** again.

I wore my **favorite** shirt in the world that day. It was blue with an **electric guitar** on the front that looked **just** like the one I have!

I was greeting all of my uncles and aunts at the party when one of them asked me a question.

"Is that your **brother's** shirt?" an aunt asked.

I felt frustrated that they assumed that since I'm a girl, I wouldn't own a shirt like this one.

But...at least she didn't call me **princess**.

"Nope, this is **mine**," I said.

After we ate and grandma blew out her candles, all of the adults sat on the couch and watched a soccer game. It was the World Cup, the **biggest** tournament around!

And my favorite team was playing, too.

I **shouted** and I jumped up and down.
My favorite team scored before halftime.

My uncle turned to me and said, "Kiara, how about you go play **dolls** with your cousin? She's playing alone."

I felt a little bit **angry** inside. They have never seen me play with a doll -- **ever!** So why would they think I'd want to do that instead?

Well...at least he didn't call me **princess**.

I didn't like playing with dolls, **not one bit**! Still, I found my cousin in the playroom where all the dolls were kept. There were **so** many different ones—tall ones and short ones with lots of **colorful** dresses lined up along the walls!

Even though the colorful dresses **sparkled** in the sunlight and looked kind of fun at first glance, I still wanted nothing more than to be up front watching the soccer game instead.

So, I set my foot down, dropped those dolls, and went to the living room to watch my **game!**

I was so excited that I got to watch my favorite team win!

But by that time, it was so late that grandma was already **snoring** on the couch.

We all said our goodbyes to each other and that's when my uncle said it...

The word that I had been **dreading** was here, waiting for me to say something back.

I knew that if I just ignored it, I would be called '**princess**' the next time I saw them,

and the **next** time,

and the **time after that**, too!

So, I decided that I had to say something about it once and for all.

"**Please** don't call me a **princess**," I said.

Suddenly, everyone was looking at me.

"I **don't** like what **princesses** like and they wouldn't like what I like either.

I like sports, I'm a gamer,

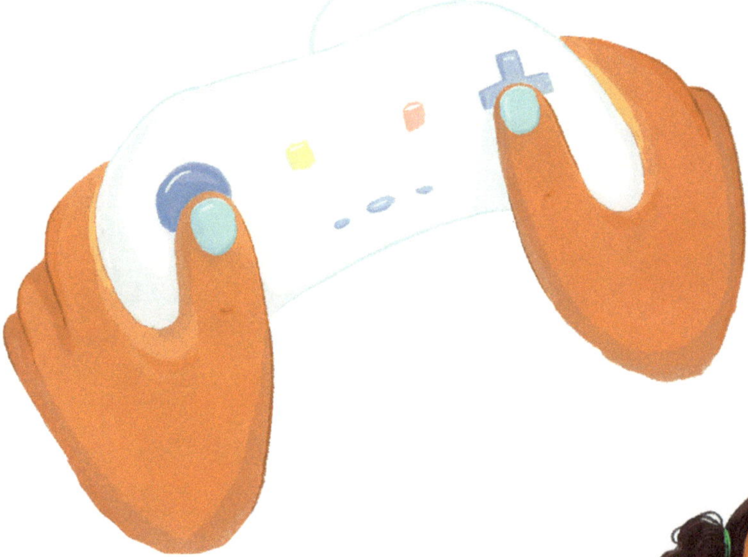

and yes, this is my favorite shirt and —

it is **not** my brother's!"

"Maybe girls don't always like girly things and that is **normal**, too. So, please, don't call me princess because that is **not** what I am.

And it would be best to not assume that other girls like being called that either," I said, full of **bravery** and **confidence**.

Everyone around me thought about it for a moment. I felt nervous, but soon smiles grew on everyone's faces. They **finally** understood.

From then on, no one in my family called me a princess **ever** again.

They didn't assume I wanted to play with dolls and they didn't buy me pink toys for the holidays. They **accepted** me for the girl I am.

I even took that bravery with me to school for career day. I stood up and told the class that I wanted to be a **police officer** just like my **aunt**.

After that, other girls waved their hands in the air to share the careers **they** wanted, too.

One wanted to be a pilot, and one wanted to be an engineer. One girl wanted to be a firefighter, and the other a scientist. It goes to show that **everyone** has different interests.

Every girl is special and unique.

There surely is not only one way to be – and the best way to be is **always to be yourself!**

If you loved this book as much as we did, there are a few ways you can help support us as authors. Leaving a review on websites like Amazon or Goodreads can help other readers find this book and decide if they want to read it.

Sharing your love for this book with your friends and family on social media can also help spread the word.

Thank you for your support, and we hope to bring you many more exciting stories in the future!

Printed in the USA
CPSIA information can be obtained
at www.ICGtesting.com
LVHW070329091123
763265LV00021B/863